Business Analytics
Step-by-Step
Tutorial

by

Narcyz Roztocki

Preface

Business Analytics refers to utilizing existing data to make business decisions. Often, however, the decision-makers lack the knowledge and skill to process the existing documents and retrieve information that is useful for their decision-making.

The objective of this tutorial is to improve basic skills on how to process existing data by providing a collection of simplified, but realistic, hands-on-examples.

In essence, this tutorial is a collection of business mini cases. It starts with relatively simple cases and then progresses step-by-step by adding complexity to each of the following business cases. Its intent is to encourage effective and efficient use of application software to help the decisions-makers. All the cases can be solved using various software packages.

Exercise 1

Carlos Gonzales is a manager at a bank. Currently, Carlos is attending a Business Analytics evening class. He has been asked to create a spreadsheet to calculate a final grade for a random student in the class. The final grade will be based on the following:

Exam 1: 25%

Exam 2: 25%

Final Exam: 25%

Homework: 20%

Class Participation: 5%

Carlos expected to design a spreadsheet for the options specified above, but the model should be able to be (re)used for future calculations. If, for example, the student specifies a new data of variables, your spreadsheet should be able to accommodate those changes and automatically provide a recalculated number. (It should assume that the model would be able to accommodate changes in all numerical parameters specified above.) In addition, it is expected to avoid any redundancy in the model.

Exam 1   50 points

Exam 2   80 points

Final Exam: 100 points

Homework   100 points

Class participation 70 points

1. What is the student's final score?
(a) 80
(b) 81
(c) 82
(d) 83
(e) None of the above

2. Assuming the following grades: Exam 1: 100 points, Exam 2: 100 points, Final Exam: 100 points, Homework: 0 points, Class participation: 100 points, what is the student's final score?
(a) 60
(b) 70
(c) 75
(d) 80
(e) None of the above

Exercise 2

Imagine you are the owner of a small construction company, which specializes in masonry and brick laying. You have been asked to create a spreadsheet to help you create a bid for a private customer who would like a wall to enclose part of their estate. You offer them two options – lava rock or brick.

Currently, you are working on the following bid:
Three workers will work three eight-hour days to build either type of wall. The wall will be 30 feet long, 5 feet tall, and 2 foot thick. Wages will be $10 per hour per person. You will have to add 25% to wages to cover fringe benefits. Lava rock will cost $4 per cubic foot. Brick will cost $2.50 per cubic foot. Your bid must add a profit margin of 40% to your total cost.

You are expected to design a spreadsheet for the two options specified above, but your model should be able to be (re)used for futures bids. If, for example, the customer specifies a new size of wall, your spreadsheet should be able to accommodate those changes and automatically provide a recalculated bid. (You should assume that your model will be able to accommodate changes in all numerical parameters specified above.) In addition, you are expected to avoid any redundancy in your model. For example, all parameters, which are applicable for both options, should be used only once.

Please Note:

A bid is a price quote, estimate, or offer. You are to create a spreadsheet model for each option (lava rock or brick) indicating a bid, which covers all costs and takes into account an overall 40 % profit margin.

1. The bid for the lava rock wall is

(a) $1,684.80
(b) $2,940.00
(c) $1,720.00
(d) $1,372.80
(e) None of the above

2. The bid for the brick wall is

(a) $1,684.80
(b) $2,310.00
(c) $1,720.00
(d) $1,372.80
(e) None of the above

3. Assuming the customer is willing to pay $3,000 (max.) for the wall. Which type of the wall can you build?

(a) Lava rock
(b) Brick wall
(c) Lava rock or Brick wall
(d) None of the above

4. Assuming the wall will be 60 feet long, 5 feet tall, and 1 foot thick. What will be the adjusted bid for the brick wall?

(a) $1,684.80
(b) $2,310.00
(c) $4,118.40
(d) $4,620.00
(e) None of the above

5. Assuming the wall will be 60 feet long, 5 feet tall, and 2 feet thick. (Now, the longer wall will require more labor.) What will be the adjusted bid for the brick wall?

(a) $1,684.80
(b) $2,310.00
(c) $4,118.40
(d) $4,620.00
(e) None of the above

Exercise 3

Jennifer, a business analyst at a large company, wishes to borrow money from her bank to buy a new car, which costs $27,000. To do this, she needs to borrow $25,000. Jen has visited her bank and they have given her the following information:

The amount to borrow will be $25,000 at 3.9% for five years.

Jen wants to know if she can afford the loan. Jen's monthly salary is $2,500, of which 20% is available for her monthly loan payments.

Create a worksheet to enter the price, the down payment, the interest rate, the term in years, as well as Jen's monthly salary along with the percentage available for her monthly loan payments. Assume that there is a down payment in the amount of $2,000.

Enter the appropriate formulas to compute the amount to finance, the maximum amount Jen can afford (20 % of the monthly salary) and the monthly loan payment.

Include an IF function that compares the monthly loan payment to the maximum she can afford and prints "YES" or "NO" depending on the answer.

You are expected to design a spreadsheet for the loan decision specified above, but your model should be able to be reused. If, for example, Jennifer whish to borrow money from her bank to buy a house, your spreadsheet should be able to accommodate those changes and automatically provide a recalculated monthly loan payment. (You should assume that your will be able to accommodate changes in all numerical parameters specified above.) In addition, you are expected to avoid any redundancy in your model

1. Jen's monthly payment will be:

(a) $459,29
(b) $896.21
(c) $1,275.46
(d) $1,994.08
(e) None of the above

Exercise 4

After working several year a business analyst for a large company in New York City, Jennifer Miller got promoted to a senior management position. Jen's promotion is associated with a substantial increase in her salary. Now, Jen wishes to buy a brand-new apartment in New York City, which costs $1,400,000. Since she is able to provide only $300,000 from her own savings, she needs to borrow the remaining $1,100,000. Jen has visited her bank and they have given her the following information:

The amount to borrow will be $1,100,000 at 4.0 % for thirty years.

Jen estimates that about 35% her new monthly salary is available for her monthly loan payments. After some calculations, Jen knows her monthly loan payments will be slightly above her limit but hopes that she still can get the loan approved and buy the apartment.

1. Jen's monthly payment will be

(a) $1,102.34
(b) $3,251.57
(c) $5,251.57
(d) $44,000.03
(e) None of the above

2. Jen's annual salary is about
(a) $80,000
(b) $120,000
(c) $180,000
(d) $250,000
(e) None of the above

Exercise 5

The demand for electricity over the period 2008 to 2014 is shown in the following table. Create a chart and calculate a regression line for the data.

Year	Electricity Demand
2008	740
2009	790
2010	800
2011	900
2012	1,050
2013	1,420
2014	1,220

1. What is your forecast for 2015?

(a) 1,210
(b) 1,310
(c) 1,420
(d) 1,520
(e) None of the above

2. What is your forecast for 2016?

(a) 1,210
(b) 1,310
(c) 1,420
(d) 1,520
(e) None of the above

Exercise 6

Carlos Gonzales is a manager at a bank. Currently, Carlos is attending a Business Analytics evening class. Now, using the tools he learned in class, Carlos likes to examine his company data.

Open the **savings-bank.txt** file located at the Business Analytics website: http://www.newpaltz.edu/~roztockn/ba.htm

1. How many employees make $75,000 or more?
(a) 23
(b) 25
(c) 27
(d) 29
(e) None of the above

2. What is the average salary for all employees in Boston?
(a) $50,000
(b) $60,000
(c) $70,000
(d) $80,000
(e) None of the above

3. How many employees are listed as "Manager"?
(a) 10
(b) 11
(c) 12
(d) 13
(e) None of the above

4. The average salary for the managers is:
(a) $80,000
(b) $100,000
(c) $120,000
(d) $140,000
(e) None of the above

5. How many employees received a bonus of $1,000.00 or higher this year?
(a) 10
(b) 12
(c) 15
(d) 18
(e) None of the above

Exercise 7

Carlos Gonzales is a manager at a bank. Currently, Carlos is attending a Business Analytics evening class. Now, using the tools he learned in class, Carlos likes to examine his company data.

Open the **savings-bank.txt** file located at the Business Analytics website:
http://www.newpaltz.edu/~roztockn/ba.htm

1. How many employees are listed as top executives ("Manager" and "Senior Account Rep")?
    (a) 10
    (b) 11
    (c) 12
    (d) 13
    (e) None of the above

2. The average salary for the managers in Boston is:
    (a) $82,000
    (b) $102,000
    (c) $122,000
    (d) $142,000
    (e) None of the above

3. How many employees in Boston received a bonus of $1,000.00 or higher this year?
    (a) 5
    (b) 7
    (c) 9
    (d) 11
    (e) None of the above

Exercise 8

Vladimir Hodinko is a business analyst at a global software development and consulting company. Recently, Vlad was asked to perform a one-hour presentation for the senior management. The executives are mostly interested in figures related to company's employees.

Open the **globalcompany.txt** file located at the Business Analytics website: http://www.newpaltz.edu/~roztockn/ba.htm

1. How many employees in the USA are listed as "Senior Manager"?
(a) 2
(b) 3
(c) 4
(d) 5
(e) none of the above

2. The GlobalCompany is present in how many countries?
(a) 18
(b) 19
(c) 20
(d) 21
(e) none of the above

3. How many employees in Chicago (USA) receive a salary of $60,000 or more?
(a) 50
(b) 53
(c) 56
(d) 59
(e) None of the above

Exercise 9

Steve is a business analyst at a manufacturing company with headquarters in Pittsburgh, Pennsylvania. Unfortunately, the financial situation of the company is not very good. To face this unfortunate situation, the company's management is planning an emergency meeting. Steve is asked to analyze the existing data.

Open the **abc-manuafacturing-company.txt** file located at the Business Analytics website: http://www.newpaltz.edu/~roztockn/ba.htm

1. How many employees in Pennsylvania (PA) receive a salary of $65,000 or more?
(a) 13
(b) 14
(c) 15
(d) 16
(e) None of the above

2. How many employees in Ohio (OH) and New York (NY) receive a salary of $85,000 or more?
(a) 17
(b) 18
(c) 19
(d) 20
(e) None of the above

Exercise 10

Steve is a business analyst at a manufacturing company with headquarters in Pittsburgh, Pennsylvania. Unfortunately, the financial situation of the company is not very good. To face this unfortunate situation, the company's management is planning an emergency meeting. Steve is asked to analyze the existing data.

Open the **abc-manuafacturing-company.txt** file located at the Business Analytics website: http://www.newpaltz.edu/~roztockn/ba.htm

1. The ABC Manufacturing Company is present at how many states?
(a) 2
(b) 3
(c) 4
(d) 5
(e) None of the above

2. How many employees receive a salary of $45,000 or more?
(a) 59
(b) 60
(c) 61
(d) 62
(e) None of the above

3. How many employees did not receive a bonus this year?
(a) 31
(b) 32
(c) 33
(d) 34
(e) None of the above

4. What is the average salary for all employees?
(a) $76,000
(b) $81,000
(c) $86,000
(d) $91,000
(e) None of the above

5. The average salary for the employees hired on or after 11/1/2001 is:
(a) $75,000
(b) $77,500
(c) $83,000
(d) $87,000
(e) None of the above

6. How many employees are listed as "CAD Drafter"?
(a) 1
(b) 2
(c) 3
(d) 4
(e) None of the above

7. How many employees are listed as managers (Group Managers, Operations Managers, Senior Managers and Sales Managers)?
(a) 15
(b) 16
(c) 17
(d) 18
(e) None of the above

8. The average salary for all the managers is:
(a) $128,235
(b) $130,556
(c) $134,556
(d) $142,235
(e) None of the above

9. What is the average salary for all employees in Toledo, OH?
(a) $76,200
(b) $78,200
(c) $80,200
(d) $90,200
(e) None of the above

10. How many employees are listed as "Manufacturing Employee"?
(a) 26
(b) 27
(c) 28
(d) 29
(e) None of the above

11. The average salary for the manufacturing employees in Cleveland, OH is:
(a) $70,500
(b) $73,500
(c) $76,500
(d) $79,500
(e) None of the above

12. The average salary for the engineers is:
(a) $69,250
(b) $79,250
(c) $89,250
(d) $99,250
(e) None of the above

13. How many employees received a bonus of $1,000.00 or higher?
(a) 25
(b) 26
(c) 27
(d) 28
(e) None of the above

14. How many employees in Indiana (IN) received a bonus of $1,000.00 or higher?
(a) 1
(b) 2
(c) 3
(d) 4
(e) None of the above

15. The lowest total employee compensations (salaries and bonuses) are in which state?
(a) Pennsylvania (PA)
(b) New York (NY)
(c) Ohio (OH)
(d) Indiana (IN)
(e) None of the above

Exercise 11

A Company is considering to build an upscale hotel near Honolulu, Hawaii. The piece of land costs $30 million. The project will take 3 years to complete and cost $20 million per year. After the construction is completed, the hotel is expected to generate $9 million per year. After ten years, the hotel (including the land) will have market value of $133 million.

1. If the company is willing to accept any capital investment that will earn at least 10 %, should the investment be considered?

(a) No.
(b) Yes.

2. The internal rate of return (IRR) for his investment is:

(a) 7 %
(b) 9 %
(c) 11 %
(d) 13 %
(e) None of the above

Exercise 12

Steve is a business analyst at a manufacturing company with headquarters in Pittsburgh, Pennsylvania. Unfortunately, the financial situation of the company is not very good. To face this unfortunate situation, the company's management is planning an emergency meeting. Steve is asked to analyze the existing data.

Open the **abc-manufacturing-company-employees.txt** file and the **abc-manuafacturing-company-employees-new.txt** file located at the Business Analytics website: http://www.newpaltz.edu/~roztockn/ba.htm

1. How many employees in Pennsylvania (PA) receive a salary of $65,000 or more?
    (a) 17
    (b) 18
    (c) 19
    (d) 20
    (e) None of the above

2. How many employees in in Ohio (OH) receive a salary of $65,000 or less?
    (a) 10
    (b) 11
    (c) 12
    (d) 13
    (e) None of the above

3. How many employees in Ohio (OH) and New York (NY) receive a salary of $85,000 or more?
    (a) 17
    (b) 18
    (c) 19
    (d) 20
    (e) None of the above

Exercise 13

Carlos Gonzales is a manager at a bank. Currently, Carlos is attending a Business Analytics evening class. Now, using the tools he learned in class, Carlos likes to examine his company data.

Open the **savings-bank-employees.txt** file and the **savings-bank-branches.txt** file located at the Business Analytics website: http://www.newpaltz.edu/~roztockn/ba.htm

1. How many employees make $75,000 or more?
(a) 23
(b) 25
(c) 27
(d) 29
(e) None of the above

2. How many employees in Boston receive a salary of $70,000 or more?
(a) 7
(b) 8
(c) 9
(d) 10
(e) None of the above

3. How many employees in California (CA) receive a salary of $80,000 or more?
(a) 8
(b) 9
(c) 10
(d) 11
(e) None of the above

Exercise 14

Jeff Bonder is an owner-manager of "Frequent Fliers," a travel agency. Jeff is planning a marketing campaign, which is intended to promote ticket sales. To better customize the marketing campaign, Jeff plans to examine the existing transaction records.

Open the **Frequent Fliers - Airports.txt** file and the **Frequent Fliers - Transactions.txt** located at the Business Analytics website: http://www.newpaltz.edu/~roztockn/ba.htm

Use the appropriate functions to answer the following questions.

1. How many sales persons work for this company?
(a) 21
(b) 23
(c) 24
(d) 25
(e) None of the above

2. Who sold the largest number of tickets?
(a) Matt
(b) Jessica
(c) Bob
(d) Ariel
(e) None of the above

3. Who sold the smallest number of tickets?
(a) Matt
(b) Jessica
(c) Bob
(d) Ariel
(e) None of the above

4. Who generated the highest revenue in ticket sales?
(a) Matt
(b) Jessica
(c) Bob
(d) Ariel
(e) None of the above

5. How many tickets did Samantha sell?
(a) 55
(b) 61
(c) 63
(d) 66
(e) None of the above

6. How much revenue in ticket sales did Samantha generate?
(a) $100,000.00
(b) $105,000.00
(c) $110,000.00
(d) $115,000.00
(e) None of the above

Exercise 15

Jeff Bonder is an owner-manager of "Frequent Fliers," a travel agency. Jeff is planning a marketing campaign, which is intended to promote ticket sales between the USA and Germany. To better customize the marketing campaign, Jeff plans to examine the existing transaction records.

Open the **Frequent Fliers - Airports.txt** file and the **Frequent Fliers - Transactions.txt** located at the BDSS website: http://www.newpaltz.edu/~roztockn/dss.htm

Use the appropriate functions to answer the following questions.

1. How many tickets were sold for flights from Germany to the USA?
(a) 12
(b) 20
(c) 30
(d) 34
(e) None of the above

2. How many tickets were sold for flights from the USA to Germany?
(a) 12
(b) 20
(c) 30
(d) 34
(e) None of the above

3. What is the average price for tickets in Business Class for flights from Germany to the USA?
(a) $5,960
(b) $6,000
(c) $9,333
(d) $29,800.00
(e) None of the above

4. What is the average price for tickets in Business Class for flights from the USA to Germany?
(a) $5,700
(b) $5,960
(c) $6,000
(d) $29,800.00
(e) None of the above

Exercise 16

Jeff Bonder is an owner-manager of "Frequent Fliers," a travel agency. After reading an article about Cote d'Azur, known as the French Riviera, Jeff considers that France presents a tremendous opportunity to sell high priced airline tickets to his well-off customers. Before starting a marketing campaign, Jeff wishes to learn more about the current status of ticket sales from the USA to France and from France to the USA.

Open the **Frequent Fliers - Airports.txt** file and the **Frequent Fliers - Transactions.txt** located at the Business Analytics website: http://www.newpaltz.edu/~roztockn/ba.htm

1. How many tickets were sold for flights from the USA to France?
(a) 18
(b) 20
(c) 25
(d) 30
(e) None of the above

2. What is the average price for tickets in First Class for flights from the USA to France?
(a) $11,200.00
(b) $11,600.00
(c) $11,800.00
(d) $12,000.00
(e) None of the above

3. How many tickets were sold for flights from France to the USA?
(a) 20
(b) 25
(c) 30
(d) 35
(e) None of the above

4. What is the average price for tickets in First Class for flights from France to the USA?
(a) $11,200.00
(b) $11,600.00
(c) $11,800.00
(d) $12,000.00
(e) None of the above

Exercise 17

After moving to New York City, Jennifer Miller decided to open her own travel agency, a move which proved to be a huge financial success. In order to use the momentum and to move her company to the next level, Jen decided to conduct an in-depth analysis of her business.

Open the **Ticket Sales - Transations.txt** file, and **Ticket Sales - Airports.txt** file located at the Business Analytics website: http://www.newpaltz.edu/~roztockn/ba.htm

1. Based on data, how many tickets were sold in November 2014?
   (a) 379
   (b) 674
   (c) 993
   (d) 1,127
   (e) None of the above

2. Based on data, how many tickets were sold to the New York City Airports (JFK, EWR and LGA)?
   (a) 437
   (b) 1,097
   (c) 1,312
   (d) 1,457
   (e) None of the above

3. Based on data, how many tickets did Samantha sell to the New York City Airports (JFK, EWR and LGA)?
   (a) 7
   (b) 10
   (c) 14
   (d) 19
   (e) None of the above

Exercise 18

After moving to New York City, Jennifer Miller decided to open her own travel agency, a move which proved to be a huge financial success. In order to use the momentum and to move her company to the next level, Jen decided to conduct an in-depth analysis of her business.

Open the **Ticket Sales - Transations.txt** file, and **Ticket Sales - Airports.txt** file located at the Business Analytics website: http://www.newpaltz.edu/~roztockn/ba.htm

1. Based on data, how many tickets were sold in total?
(a) 9,307
(b) 9,907
(c) 10,300
(d) 11,495
(e) None of the above

2. Based on data, what was the average number of tickets sold per transition?
(a) 1.8
(b) 2.2
(c) 2.6
(d) 3.0
(e) None of the above

3. Based on data, how many sales representatives ware working for this company?
(a) 47
(b) 52
(c) 57
(d) 62
(e) None of the above

4. Who sold the most tickets?
(a) Alexandra
(b) Brandon
(c) Stanislava
(d) Bob
(e) None of the above

5. Who sold the least tickets?
(a) Jessica
(b) Sam
(c) Amy
(d) Ariel
(e) None of the above

6. Based on data, how many tickets were sold in the third quarter?
(a) 1,014
(b) 1,096
(c) 2,813
(d) 3,127
(e) None of the above

7. Based on data, how many tickets were sold to Germany?
(a)　697
(b) 1,082
(c) 1,312
(d) 1,457
(e) None of the above

8. Based on data, how many tickets did Jessica sell to China?
(a) 12
(b) 13
(c) 37
(d) 39
(e) None of the above

9. Based on data, what are the four most popular destinations?
(a) USA, China, Germany, Poland
(b) USA, China, France, Canada
(c) USA, Germany, France, Ireland
(d) USA, Canada, Poland, Japan
(e) None of the above

10. Based on data, what are the two least popular destinations?
(a) United Arab Emirates, Hungary
(b) Hungary, Ireland
(c) United Arab Emirates, Ireland
(d) France, Canada
(e) None of the above

Exercise 19

Jeff Bonder is an owner-manager of "Frequent Fliers," a travel agency. After reading an article about China, Jeff believes that travel to this emerging economy presents a lucrative opportunity to offer tickets, in particular, to business travelers. Jeff seeks to examine the existing data to learn more about his current ticket sales to China.

Open the **Frequent Fliers - Airports.txt** file, the **Frequent Fliers - Transactions.txt** file, and the **Frequent Fliers – Transactions 3.txt** located at the at the Business Analytics website: http://www.newpaltz.edu/~roztockn/ba.htm

Use the appropriate functions to answer the following questions.

1. How many tickets in Business Class were sold for flights from the USA to China?
   (a) 13
   (b) 24
   (c) 37
   (d) 109
   (e) None of the above

2. What is the average price for tickets in Business Class for flights from the USA to China?
   (a) $2,200.00
   (b) $2,339.17
   (c) $2,363.08
   (d) $2,800.00
   (e) None of the above

3. How many tickets in Business Class were sold for flights from China to the USA?
   (a) 13
   (b) 24
   (c) 37
   (d) 109
   (e) None of the above

4. What is the average price for tickets in Business Class for flights from China to the USA?
   (a) $2,200.00
   (b) $2,339.17
   (c) $2,363.08
   (d) $2,800.00
   (e) None of the above

Exercise 20

Jeff Bonder is an owner-manager of "Frequent Fliers," a travel agency. To improve the business performance of his company, Jeff likes to know about the past performance of his team.

Open the **Frequent Fliers - Airports.txt** file, the **Frequent Fliers – Sales Agents.txt** file, the **Frequent Fliers – Sales Offices.txt** file, the **Frequent Fliers – Transactions.txt** and the **Frequent Fliers – Transactions 3.txt** located on the Business Analytics website: http://www.newpaltz.edu/~roztockn/ba.htm

Use the appropriate functions to answer the following questions.

1. Which sales office sold the largest number of tickets?
(a) Hoboken
(b) Kingston
(c) Albany
(d) Jersey City
(e) None of the above

2. Which sales office sold the smallest number of tickets?
(a) Hoboken
(b) Kingston
(c) Albany
(d) Jersey City
(e) None of the above

3. How many tickets did the sales office in New Paltz sell?
(a) 206
(b) 90
(c) 59
(d) 26
(e) None of the above

4. How many tickets did the sales office in Jersey City sell?
(a) 206
(b) 90
(c) 59
(d) 26
(e) None of the above

5. How many tickets for flights from the USA to France did the sales office in New Paltz sell?
(a) 0
(b) 1
(c) 2
(d) 3
(e) None of the above

6. Which sales office sold the largest number of tickets in the business class?
(a) Hoboken
(b) Kingston
(c) Albany
(d) Jersey City
(e) None of the above

7. Which sales office sold the smallest number of tickets in the business class?
(a) Hoboken
(b) Kingston
(c) Albany
(d) Jersey City
(e) None of the above

8. What was the average price of tickets sold by the sales office in New Paltz, rounded to the nearest dollar?
(a) $1276
(b) $1776
(c) $2276
(d) $2812
(e) None of the above

Exercise 21

Jeff Bonder is an owner-manager of "Frequent Fliers," a travel agency. To improve the business performance of his company, Jeff likes to know more about the buying patterns of his customers.

Open the **Frequent Fliers - Airports.txt** file, the **Frequent Fliers – Transactions 3.txt**, the **Frequent Fliers – Transactions 4.txt**, the **Frequent Fliers – Transactions 5.txt**, the **Frequent Fliers - Sales Agents.txt, Frequent Fliers - Sales Offices.txt**, the **Frequent Fliers - Members.txt, the Frequent Fliers - Members - Transactions 3.txt, the Frequent Fliers - Members - Transactions 4.txt and the Frequent Fliers - Members - Transactions 5.txt** on the Business Analytics website: http://www.newpaltz.edu/~roztockn/ba.htm

1. Compute the mean for all tickets concerning General Members. Based on the data, what is the average for all tickets bought by General Members rounded to the nearest dollar?
A) $1,700
B) $2,358
C) $2,878
D) $3,073
E) None of the above

2. Compute the mean for all tickets concerning Silver Members. Based on the data, what is the average for all tickets bought by Silver Members rounded to the nearest dollar?
A) $1,700
B) $2,358
C) $2,878
D) $3,073
E) None of the above

3) Compute the median for all tickets concerning Silver Members. Based on the data, what is the median price for all tickets bought by Silver Members rounded to the nearest dollar?
A) $1,700
B) $2,358
C) $2,878
D) $3,073
E) None of the above

4) Compute the standard deviation for all tickets concerning Silver Members. Based on the data, what is the standard deviation for all tickets bought by Silver Members, rounded to the nearest dollar?
A) $190
B) $3,465
C) $16,310
D) $16,500
E) None of the above

5) Compute the range for all tickets concerning Silver Members. Based on the data, what is the range for all tickets bought by Silver Members, rounded to the nearest dollar?
A) $190
B) $3,465
C) $16,310
D) $16,500
E) None of the above

Exercise 22

Jeff Bonder is an owner-manager of "Frequent Fliers," a travel agency. To improve the business performance of his company, Jeff likes to know more about the buying patterns of his customers.

Open the **Frequent Fliers - Airports.txt** file, the **Frequent Fliers – Transactions 3.txt,** the **Frequent Fliers – Transactions 4.txt,** the **Frequent Fliers – Transactions 5.txt,** the **Frequent Fliers - Sales Agents.txt, Frequent Fliers - Sales Offices.txt,** the **Frequent Fliers - Members.txt,** the **Frequent Fliers - Members - Transactions 3.txt,** the **Frequent Fliers - Members - Transactions 4.txt and the Frequent Fliers - Members - Transactions 5.txt** located on the Business Analytics website: http://www.newpaltz.edu/~roztockn/ba.htm

1. In total, how much did Pauline (271053;Leblanc,Pauline) spend on her tickets?
A) $3,550
B) $6,185
C) $24,740
D) $51,740
E) None of the above

2. What is the computed mean for all of the tickets Pauline (271053;Leblanc,Pauline) bought?
A) $3,550
B) $6,185
C) $24,740
D) $51,740
E) None of the above

3. How many tickets did Pauline (271053;Leblanc,Pauline) buy in total?
A) 1
B) 2
C) 3
D) 4
E) None of the above

4. In which office(s) did Pauline (271053;Leblanc,Pauline) purchase her tickets?
A) Kingston
B) Trenton
C) Kingston, Newark and Trenton
D) Kingston, New Paltz, Newark and Trenton
E) None of the above

5. Based on the records, which countries did Pauline (271053;Leblanc,Pauline) visit?
A) Australia and USA
B) France, Germany and USA
C) Australia, France, and USA
D) Australia, France, Germany and USA
E) None of the above

Answers

Exercise 1
1. b
2. d

Exercise 2
1. b
2. b
3. c
4. b
5. d

Exercise 3
1. a

Exercise 4
1. c
2. c

Exercise 5
1. c
2. d

Exercise 6
1. c
2. d
3. b
4. c
5. c

Exercise 7
1. c
2. c
3. b

Exercise 8
1. b
2. c
3. b

Exercise 9
1. a
2. b

Exercise 10
1. c
2. b
3. b

4. c
5. b
6. a
7. d
8. c
9. b
10. c
11. b
12. a
13. d
14. a
15. d

Exercise 11
1. b
2. c

Exercise 12
1. a
2. a
3. b

Exercise 13
1. c
2. c
3. a

Exercise 14
1. c
2. b
3. d
4. b
5. b
6. c

Exercise 15
1. d
2. a
3. a
4. a

Exercise 16
1. a
2. b
3. c
4. a

Exercise 17
1. c
2. b
3. c

Exercise 18
1. d
2. c
3. c
4. c
5. b
6. c
7. b
8. d
9. a
10. c

Exercise 19
1. b
2. b
3. a
4. c

Exercise 20
1. a
2. d
3. b
4. d
5. c
6. e
7. d
8. c

Exercise 21
1. b
2. d
3. a
4. b
5. c

Exercise 22
1. c
2. b
3. d
4. c
5. d

www.ingramcontent.com/pod-product-compliance
Lightning Source LLC
Chambersburg PA
CBHW021853170526
45157CB00006B/2424